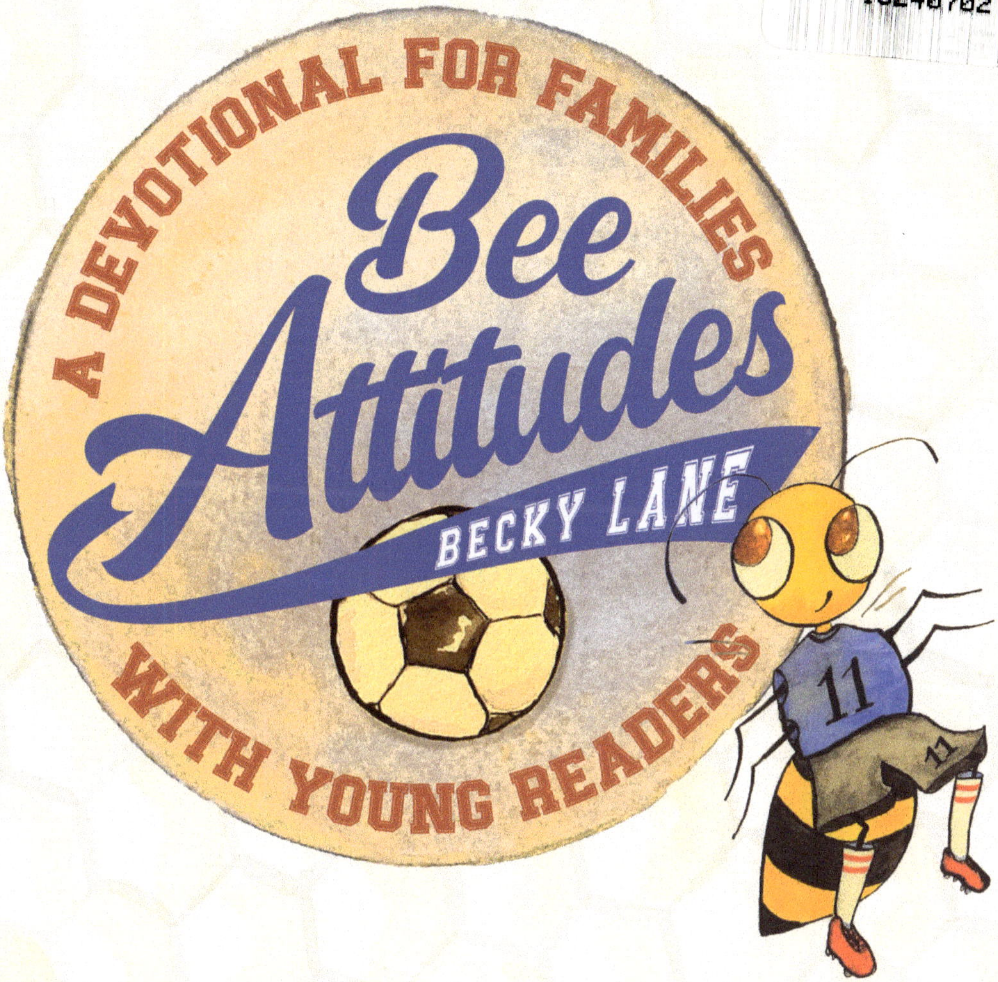

Bee Attitudes

A Devotional for Families with Young Readers

Becky Lane

Ambassador International
Greenville, South Carolina & Belfast, Northern Ireland

www.ambassador-international.com

Bee Attitudes
A DEVOTIONAL FOR FAMILIES WITH YOUNG READERS

©2025 by Becky Lane

All rights reserved. This book or any portion thereof may not be reproduced or used in any manner whatsoever without the express written permission of the author and publisher, except for the use of brief quotations in a book review.

ISBN: 978-1-64960-516-0, hardcover

ISBN: 978-1-64960-515-3, paperback

eISBN: 978-1-64960-558-0

Scripture quotations are taken from the Holy Bible, New International Version®, NIV Copyright 1973, 1978, 1984, 2011

Edited by Katie Cruice Smith
Illustrated by Becky Lane
Cover Design by Karen Slayne
Digital Edition by Anna Riebe Raats

AMBASSADOR INTERNATIONAL
Emerald House
411 University Ridge, Suite B14
Greenville, SC. 29601
www.ambassador-international.com

AMBASSADOR INTERNATIONAL BOOKS
The Mount
2 Woodstock Link
Belfast, BT6 8DD, Northern Ireland, UK
www.ambassadormedia.co.uk

The colophon is a trademark of Ambassador, a Christian publishing company.

Dear Parents,

This book is meant to be read and discussed as a family. You are your child's first and most important teacher. Deuteronomy 6:6-9 makes this clear. Being with you, your child will learn so much. My hope is that this book will spark conversations of God's love.

Bolded words are explained at the end of the book in Granddad's Glossary. Feel free to fly there if your child needs to know what a word means.

Sincerely,
Becky Lane

"But the meek will inherit the land and enjoy peace and prosperity"
Psalm 37:11

To Roselina
If bees could tell stories, they would be worth hearing.

Deanna
thank you for using your scholarly skills to make this book better.

Pastor Bryan
thank you for challenging me to keep pursuing writing.

Mr. Lightfoot
your teacher wisdom and creativity are a blessing.

Mom and Dad
thank you for always pointing us to Jesus.

Melanie
you've always been the best cheerleader!

Day 1
BLESSED
Psalm 103:2

Bennett practiced . . .

And in the game, he failed.

Bennett practiced more . . .

But still, he failed.

"I can't do this."

Bennett practiced again . . . and again . . . and again.

He failed . . . and failed . . . and failed.

"I won't ever be able to do this!
Winning is everything, and I'll never win."
He started pulling a poster off his wall.

Granddad saw what was happening.
"You've been practicing so hard.
I'm proud of you. You are a **blessing**."

Bennett said, "How can I be a blessing?
I'm not the best. I'm not even very good."

"You are a blessing to me," Granddad said.

"What is a blessing, anyway?"

"A blessing is a gift. To be **blessed** is to be special, set apart."

"I don't want to be special! I want to win! I was set apart enough today," Bennett said.

"There's more to life than winning a game."

"I know. I want to win a trophy!" Bennett threw his poster on the floor.

1. Have you ever felt like Bennett? Does it feel like no matter how hard you try, you'll never get things right? What do you do about it?

2. It is important to not forget all the good things God does. Someone like Granddad can help us remember. Who can you talk to when things are hard?

3. Feelings are given to us by God, and He puts people in our lives to help us. We can help others as well. Can you think of a way you could help someone?

Did You Know?

All through the Bible, God blesses His people. He gives good gifts. Deuteronomy 28:2 says, "All these blessings will come on you and accompany you if you obey the Lord your God."

Day 2
BEE ATTITUDES
Matthew 5:1-2

Granddad picked up the crumpled poster. "Let me tell you a story. Once there was a swarm of bees that lived not far from Galilee. Each one was very much like the others. They each had two antennae, six legs, and certainly two sets of specially designed wings."

Bennett made a face.
"Granddad, is this a kids' story?"

Granddad said, "It may sound like a kids' story, but you can learn something from it, too. This is a story about my great-great-very-great-granddad when he climbed the mountain."

"The one where the olives grow? We do that every spring when the blossoms come."

"A Man was there with a crowd swarming around Him. My granddad wanted to know what was happening, so he flew over."

Bennett was puzzled. "Didn't the crowd scare him away?"

"No, they were too busy listening to the Man."

"What did He say? It must have been important."

"The Man talked about what humans today call the **Beatitudes**."

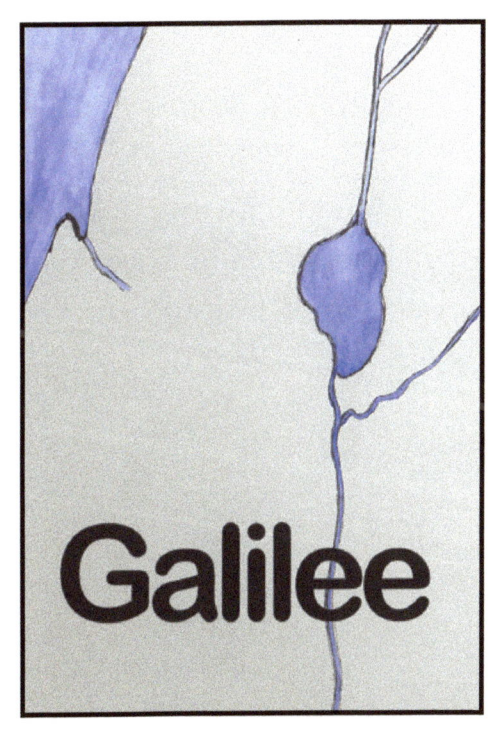

"What are *bee* attitudes? Granddad, I don't know what an attitude is! How am I supposed to have one?"

"The words sound the same, but they are not. An attitude is like a feeling or a thought that affects you and others around you. An attitude can be a good thing or a bad thing. Every bee has an **attitude**."

"Well, then, so do dragonflies!" Bennett interrupted. "I don't know why you are telling me that. The Daring Dragonflies were not showing good attitudes today, and they won."

"All of us, big and small, have attitudes," Granddad said.

"I still don't know why humans would care about our attitudes."

"The Man in our story talked about something very important. The special word for each thing He talked about is 'beatitude.' It just sounds like 'bee' and the word 'attitude' stuck together."

"Oh. Then what is a beatitude?"

"A beatitude is a **quality** that we should have. It teaches us to respond to things the way God would want us to, rather than our own way."

1. Sometimes, our attitudes change. We don't always get what we want. What kind of attitudes have you seen?

2. Parents are called to talk to their children about God and tell His stories! Look at Deuteronomy 6:5-7: "Love the LORD your God with all your heart and with all your soul and with all your strength. These commandments that I give you today are to be on your hearts. Impress them on your children. Talk about them when you sit at home and when you walk along the road, when you lie down and when you get up."

LISTEN TO IMPORTANT STORIES

Did You Know?

Plants can't do things alone, and neither can we. Plants produce a powdery substance called **pollen**. In order to make fruit and seeds, grains of pollen in a flower need to transfer from the anther to the stigma to create new seeds. Take a look at the illustration. Animals and insects can collect the pollen for food. We need pollinators, like bees, to have most fruits and vegetables. Wind can also help plants produce fruit. Olive trees are mostly pollinated by wind.

Day 3
CRYING CHEERLEADERS
Matthew 5:3

Bennett yelled at his teammates, "Get it together!"

Penelopbee told the other cheerleaders, "Maybe we will win!"

"Be aggressive. Bee, be aggressive!" they shouted.

The cheerleaders' job was to help keep everyone's spirits high, but their team lost again.

They did their last cheer; Penelopbee started crying, and so did some others.

That made Bennett more upset.

After the game, Granddad took Bennett out to eat. Bennett wasn't very hungry at Honey's Pizza Shop.

"It is hard to lose. I've lost many games, too," Granddad said.

Bennett sighed and sipped his drink.
"Can you tell me more of the story?"

"The Man said,
'**Blessed** are the poor in spirit,
for theirs is the kingdom of heaven.'"

Bennett asked, "What do you mean, 'poor in spirit'?"

"What does it mean to be poor?"

"To not have much honey."

"Or poor can just mean that you do not have much. The Man was saying that those who don't have much spirit but are **humbled** by God's **grace** are special to Him—so special that they are **citizens** of **Heaven.**"

1. Being poor in spirit is the result of receiving God's grace. It means you are different from the world. How do citizens of Heaven live their lives?

2. When someone shows you kindness, how do you respond?

Did You Know?

The Beatitudes are found in Matthew 5:1-12. Jesus saw the crowds of people and sat down to teach them on the side of a mountain. The crowds of people were from many places because news about Jesus was spreading as He taught, preached, and healed people with every kind of sickness in Galilee. You and your family can read more about this in Matthew 4:23-25.

Day 4
COMFORT
Matthew 5:4

Bennett practiced . . . and failed with **frustration**.
"I can't do this. No one will ever want to be my real friend because winning is everything. All I can do is fail."
He took a deep breath. "What would a citizen of Heaven do?"
He hoped no one heard him.

Granddad visited. They had lemonade and cookies together while they watched a soccer match.

Bennett took the last cookie. When Granddad asked where his last cookie went, Bennett said his sister, Bea, took it. Next, their favorite team lost, and Bennett felt like he wanted to hide. Then he remembered the story.

"Granddad, did the Man in your beatitude story say anything else?"

"'Blessed are those who **mourn**, for they will be **comforted**.'"

"Like when Dad helps me up and gives me a hug when I fall?"

"Right. God has **compassion**. He comforts those who are His."

"I've been having a bad day."

"The beatitude is not just for bad days or when you feel like you are alone. Comfort God gives is for when you know you've done something wrong and you want to fix the problem."

Bennett knew compassion from his family. What would it look like to be comforted by God?

"Granddad, I ate the last cookie, not Bea," he said with his head down.
"I feel terrible. I lied, and it feels worse than our team losing.
Will you forgive me, please?"
Granddad hugged him. "I gladly forgive you."

1. Have you ever felt like no one will want to be your friend because you are not good enough? What did you do about it?

2. When we feel down, our family can be a great comfort to us. How has your family comforted you?

3. The biggest thing to mourn over is sin. The greatest comfort is knowing God's forgiveness. How has your family been comforted by God?

TRUE MOURNING BRINGS REAL COMFORT

Did You Know?

The New Testament of the Bible was originally written in Greek. The word "blessed" in Matthew 5 could also be translated "happy." The Greek word is  (makarios). It's more than a feeling, though, because we can be blessed no matter what's happening around us.

Day 5
BEE HUMBLE
Matthew 5:5

Again, Bennett practiced, and he thought about being a citizen of Heaven. His team still lost.

"I can't do this! I practice, but we fail! I'll never be able to do this. I'll never win."

Bennett sat on his soccer ball until it was time to go to Beatrice's Ice Cream Parlor with the team.

He stared at the wall with photos of the teams and their trophies. His own team was quiet.

Granddad landed beside him. "Bennett, do you remember the soccer game we watched yesterday? How did it make you feel when that player looked at the camera and told everyone how wonderful he was?"

"That was just mean. He said even if he were on a different team and only he knew how to play, his skills would turn the team into winners."

"It bothered me, too. It's fine to want to be good at something, but we don't need to act like that. There's actually a beatitude for this. *'Blessed are the **meek**, for they will **inherit** the earth.'*"

"So, the Man said that weak people have the earth? That does not make sense!" Bennett said.

"Not weak people, meek people," Granddad explained. "To be meek means to be **humble**, not stuck up about what you can do. Being humble also means being thankful for our talents. God gives talents to everyone. Knowing our talents come from God and being thankful to Him is being meek. Being humble isn't easy, but it is right."

1. When have you heard people bragging? Is there something you want to brag about?

2. It is possible to have amazing skills and not be proud. When Jesus tells us to be humble, He knows what it means! God's Son left Heaven's **glory** to come down to earth to rescue us! If you and your family want to read more about that together, check out Philippians 2, especially verses four through eleven.

3. Why is being humble so hard? What do you think it means to be humbled by God's grace?

Did You Know?

The Latin root for the word "humble" is *humus*. That means "ground" or "earth." If someone is "down to earth," it means they are not stuck up (proud).

Day 6
HUNGRY AND THIRSTY
Matthew 5:6

As Bennett practiced, he thought about being humble and being comforted. He wanted to live like a citizen of Heaven.

Penelopbee told Bennett, "You've been doing a great job at practice and in the games. What's different?"

"Yeah," Pete the goalie said. "It's like you're a new bee!"

"That's what I was thinking!" Penelopbee said. "You used to get so angry at yourself and other people. You are calmer now."

"And a better player, too!" Pete said.

Bennett blushed. "My granddad has been telling me a story about a Man Who talked about the Beatitudes."

Penelopbee asked, "Why would someone talk about a bee's attitudes?"

"I wanted to know the same thing! Granddad explained that 'beatitude' just sounds like the words 'bee' and 'attitude' stuck together. He said it's actually a feature we should have. A beatitude teaches us to react to things in life the way God wants us to."

"Instead of our own way?" Pete asked.

"Right!"

Game time arrived, and they won! It would have been easy for Bennett to start buzzing about how great he and his team did, but he knew what it felt like to be on the team that lost. Would it be right for him to do that?

Granddad came up to him after the game and said, "*'Blessed are those who hunger and thirst for **righteousness**, for they will be filled.'*"

"Granddad, what does that mean?"

"Aren't you always hungry after a game?"

"Yes."

"You need to drink a lot of water, too. Why?"

"I play so hard and fly so fast that I get worn out. When I finally get a drink, it feels so good."

"The same is true with righteousness. Only God can cause such a hunger for what is right and also fill it. You will be filled when what is right finally happens."

"The referees try to do that, don't they?" Bennett asked.

"We sure do! It's a hard job!" a referee, who happened to be passing by, said.

Granddad smiled. "We naturally don't want the referee to catch us doing wrong, just other people."

1. Our bodies feel hungry because we need to eat. Did you know your spirit can be hungry, too?

2. "Righteousness" is a big word. It means to do right. Only Jesus is **righteous** all the time. When have you hungered or longed for righteousness?

Did You Know?

Words can have parts. A word's ending is called a suffix. The suffix *ness* means "a quality or state." If the sky is bright, I could say, "The sky's brightness made me wish for sunglasses."

Day 7
KIND OR MEAN
Matthew 5:7

Bennett got the ball, interrupting the play his coach called. C.J., number seventeen of the **rival** team, intercepted. Pete, the bee's goalie, couldn't block C.J.'s game-winning kick.

Nate, number five on Bennett's team, told Pete, "You don't even know how to play!"

Flustered, Bennett focused his anger on others. He told Granddad, "It's not my fault that we didn't win out there! Pete isn't a very good goalie. If he was, they wouldn't have scored on us so much."

"Is one goalie the whole team now?" Granddad asked.

"No, of course not! I'm angry. That's not how I wanted the game to go."

"'*Blessed are the **merciful**, for they will be shown **mercy**.*' Those who know God show mercy because they have received it from God. Do you understand?"

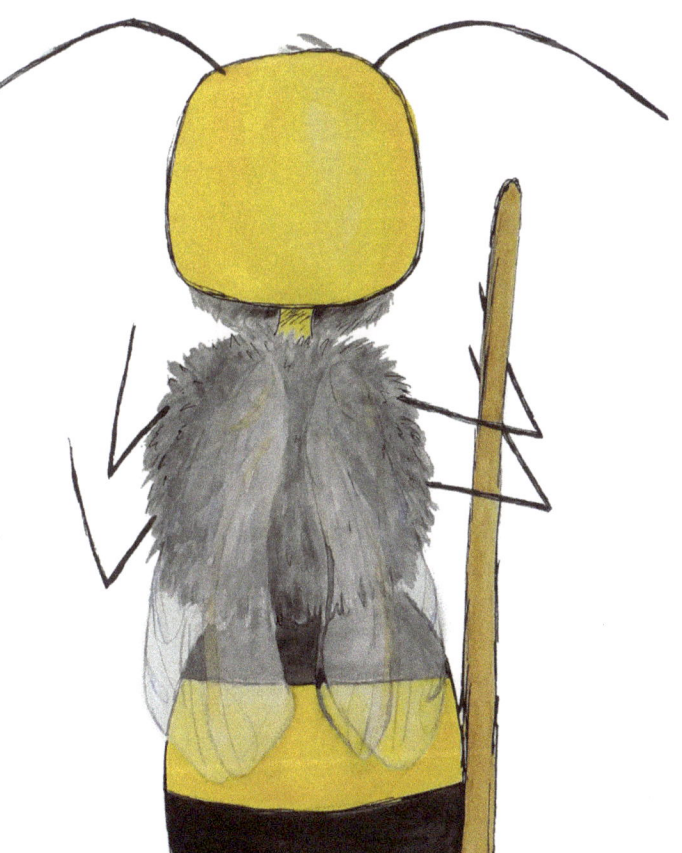

"Not really," Bennett said.

"Perhaps another way to say it would be, 'Blessed are those who are kind to others when they don't deserve it, for they will be shown kindness, too.'"

They overheard Pete tell Nate,
"Nice job in the game today."

Bennett was wide-eyed.
"Granddad, how can Pete be so kind
after Nate said mean things to him?
Everyone heard it."

Before Granddad could answer,
they heard Pete again. This time,
he was talking to James, number twenty-eight.

"Sorry I didn't do well in the game. Maybe I shouldn't have played."

"No! If you hadn't been there, the Dragonflies
would have scored even more."

"Did you see that?" Granddad asked Bennett.
"Pete, your goalie, encouraged his
teammate Nate, even though that same
bee made fun of him in the game.
Soon, a teammate encouraged
him, too!"

1. Being kind, even when someone doesn't deserve it, shows mercy. That's what God does and calls His people to do. Have you ever responded like Bennett? Did you know you made mistakes but complained about what other people did wrong instead?

2. When has someone shown you mercy? How did it make you feel? If we want to receive mercy, we should also show mercy. What is one way you show mercy to someone else?

Did You Know?

When Moses went up to Mount Sinai with the second two tablets of stone, God came down in a cloud. Here is what God said about Himself in Exodus 34:6: "'The LORD, the LORD, the compassionate and gracious God, slow to anger, abounding in love and faithfulness." God is merciful. No wonder He calls His children to be merciful.

Day 8
CLEAN
Matthew 5:8

Bennett practiced soccer and hoped to improve his kindness skills. He wasn't very happy with himself.

"Granddad, what can I do? After the game the other day, I was so mad at Pete. I said I was sorry, and he said he forgives me. But I don't feel forgiven. I feel dirty."

"*'Blessed are the **pure** in heart, for they will see God.'* God looks at the heart. That's where our attitudes and actions come from. If we know His love, we are filled with love for Him. He makes us new. Obeying God comes from the heart.

"I have a gift for you!" Granddad tossed a soccer ball to Bennett, who tried to bounce it off his head. It thumped and plopped to the ground instead.

Bennett was a little surprised. He politely said,
"You'll need to inflate a new ball before you can use it."

"You're right. Without being inflated,
the ball can't do what it's made for," Granddad said.

"That's how I feel right now. I'm trying so hard
but still feel like I mess up too much."

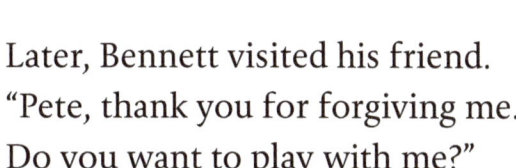

Later, Bennett visited his friend.
"Pete, thank you for forgiving me.
Do you want to play with me?"

"Sure!" Pete said.

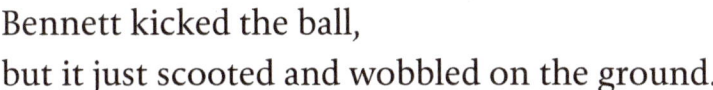

Bennett kicked the ball,
but it just scooted and wobbled on the ground.

"I think we'd better inflate that ball before we try to use it," Pete said.

"Well, that's just it. I'm like that ball. I'm kind of useless because of my attitude.
I've been trying to be kinder and do good things on my own."

"And it ended up not working well. I think that's because you didn't change
from the inside."

1. Do you try to get things right? What makes you feel like stopping?

2. It is very hard to change how we treat people without changing from the inside. The bees in our story might not fully understand this, but your family does. We need God to work in our hearts! He's ready to help. We just need to ask.

3. What clues have you seen that someone is changing from the heart?

Did You Know?

The sport Bennett plays is called football in most countries. Some children make their own soccer balls (or footballs) using old newspaper and many plastic bags tied around one another. With your parents' help, you could try this recycling project.

Day 9
MAKE IT RIGHT
Matthew 5:9

Bennett kicked the soccer ball. It glided through the air, went through an open window, and splatted on a freshly baked cake.

"You are in so much trouble!" Nate shouted as he buzzed away.

Pete and Bennett looked at each other.

Bennett whispered, "Miss Haylee is not going to be happy."

"I know, but we can't just run away," Pete said.

They rang her doorbell.

"Miss Haylee, we were practicing too close to your house," Bennett said.

"We're sorry for the mess we made," Pete told her.

"May we come in and clean it up, please?"

After they finished, Bennett visited Granddad.
"Did you hear about the mess we made today?"

"Yes. Miss Haylee called. What happened reminds me of another beatitude. *'Blessed are the **peacemakers**, for they will be called children of God.'"*

"I'm not sure I understand."

"What does your team do at the end of every game?"

Bennett pictured his team and the Daring Dragonflies. "We shake hands with the other team, and it's not always easy to do."

"Why do you shake their hands, then?"

"To make sure we get along and say, 'Good game.'"

"Those words sound amazing with all the voices. That time helps you make **peace**. Children of God are those who are at peace with God."

Bennett practiced. In the game, he sometimes failed, but he thought about the stories Granddad told him.

"I can't do this yet; but someday, I'll be able to." He worked on living like a citizen of Heaven, on and off the soccer field.

1. Soccer rivals are not the only people we might have a hard time with. Getting along with people is challenging. Jesus calls us to love our enemies (Matt. 5:43-44). God will help us! Romans 12:18 tells us that we are to seek to live at peace with everyone, "as far as it depends on [us]." How can you get along better with others?

2. Who is someone you have a hard time getting along with? What is one way you can practice being a peacemaker? If you need some ideas, be sure to talk to your family about it. We can also pray and talk to God about it!

Did You Know?

Peacemakers may not be the people you expect. Samaritans were people the Israelites did not like. Jesus told a parable about an Israelite who was robbed and badly hurt. A Samaritan took care of the hurt Israelite when the important Israelites wouldn't. Not only did the Samaritan check on the hurt Israelite, but he also made sure his needs were met. Check out Luke 10:30-37.

Day 10
BULLIED
Matthew 5:10-12

Someone got knocked over from the other team.
No one noticed, except Bennett.
He knelt down and helped the
dragonfly back to his feet.

Then bugs started to notice.
The rival team mocked him.
"I can't believe he's helping that insect up!"

"Ha! As if our team needs help."

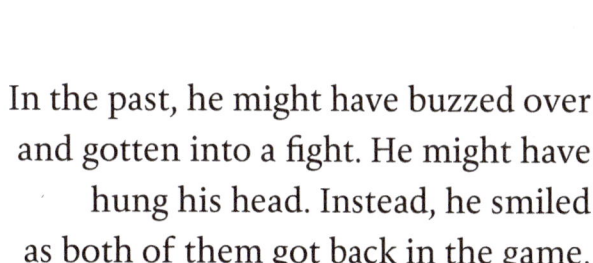

In the past, he might have buzzed over and gotten into a fight. He might have hung his head. Instead, he smiled as both of them got back in the game.

"Bennett, you are a blessing!" Granddad told him after the game. "The Man in our story also said, 'Blessed are those who are **persecuted** because of righteousness, for theirs is the kingdom of **heaven**. Blessed are you when people insult you, persecute you and falsely say all kinds of evil against you because of me. Rejoice and be glad, because great is your reward in heaven, for in the same way they persecuted the prophets who were before you.'"

"What does that mean?"

"Doing good is not wrong. There is no law against it. Some people will be hurt and even harmed for doing what is right because it shows that they are actually part of God's family and not from around here. God sees everything and will bless those who do right."

"Who was this Man?"

"His name is Jesus."

"I need Jesus to help me."

Bennett and his team weren't exactly all-stars, but he learned that he could be a blessing on or off the soccer field.

1. Have you ever noticed someone needed help? What did you do?

2. Sometimes, we hesitate to do the right thing and help because others might make fun of us. We can ask Jesus to help us do what is right and not worry about what people say or do. Have you ever had someone make fun of you for doing right? What was your response?

3. God wants us to speak up for people who cannot speak for themselves. Read and talk about Proverbs 31:8-9 as a family.

Did You Know?

Shadrach, Meshach, and Abednego loved and trusted God. They refused to bow down to an idol and, at the king's command, were thrown into a blazing furnace. The king was amazed when he saw four men walking around in the furnace and called Shadrach, Meshach, and Abednego to come out. They didn't even smell like smoke! To read more about this, check out Daniel 3.

MORE TO THINK ABOUT

Bennett and Granddad talked about what it means to be children of God. Do you know what it means? All humans are created in God's image, but there is only one way for us to be at peace with God. He always plays by the rules, and not everyone likes that.

A person who has done anything wrong, even told one lie, does not have peace with God. The Bible tells us in Romans 3:23 that each of us have **sinned** (done or thought wrong) against God, the Creator of all things, when we choose our ways instead of His. He is **just**. He must punish **sin**. Romans 6:23 tells us, "The **wages** of sin is death."

Jesus Christ, God's Son, never sinned. He chose to die on a cross to pay the fine for your sin! He took your **punishment!** He is alive today. "If we confess our sins, he is faithful and just and will **forgive** us our sins and **purify** us from all unrighteousness" (I John 1:9). That means anyone who **repents** and believes on Christ Jesus is saved! The **relationship** with God is **restored** (fixed)! Only through Jesus can we have peace with God! "For the wages of sin is death, but the gift of God is **eternal** life in Christ Jesus our Lord" (Rom. 6:23).

1. Have you asked Jesus to forgive your sins? Why?

2. Have you told others about what Jesus did? Now is a great time to talk to you family about it!

Did You Know?

The Bible talks about honey many times. God's Word is even sweeter than honey! "How sweet are your words to my taste, sweeter than honey to my mouth!" (Psalm 119:103).

Fun Facts About Bees

1. Bees have two sets of wings. When they fly, bees connect their upper and lower wings! Then, it is as if they have just one set of wings. Entering their hive, they are able to fold their wings in and take up less space. In flight, they move their wings at 230 beats per second.

2. Bees have five eyes, three of which help them understand where the horizon is. The three simple eyes are called ocelli.

3. Honeybees have been taken to outer space. The first time was in 1982.

4. Honeycomb, where bees live and store things, is made with countless hexagons.

Fun Facts about Soccer

1. Soccer is the most popular sport in the world because it has both the most fans and participants.

2 The first World Cup tournament was in Uruguay in 1930. It has been held every four years since, except in 1942 and 1946 because of World War II.

3. In 1969, El Salvador and Honduras competed for a chance to make the World Cup. The countries were at war within weeks of El Salvador's victory.

4. The classic soccer ball design with black hexagons and white pentagons was made by Adidas for the 1970 World Cup. It was designed to be easier to control, be more durable, and stand out on television. The ball was called Telstar because it would be the television "star."

GRANDDAD'S GLOSSARY

Attitude: a feeling or thought that affects you and others around you

Beatitude: a blessing given by Jesus in the Sermon on the Mount as He taught His disciples to respond to situations the way God wants rather than the way we would on our own

Blessed: special, set apart

Blessing: something positive spoken over you; something good received; being a help and positive influence for someone

Citizen: a person from a particular country, nation, or place

Comforted: to be calmed

Compassion: to care about someone and show kindness to them, especially when they go through something hard

Eternal: lasting forever and ever

Forgive: willing to be in a good relationship again after someone did something wrong

Frustration: to be very upset because you know something is not right

Glory: honor, beauty, magnificence

Grace: an undeserved gift

Heaven: the place where God the Father is, where Jesus is preparing a place for His disciples; home for the believer in Christ

Humble: not stuck up about what you can do

Inherit: to receive from the one it belonged to

Just: lawful, right, and true

Meek: to be humble about oneself, including what one is able to do

Merciful: having the quality of giving mercy

Mercy: not getting the punishment you earned because someone else took your punishment for you

Mourn: to be very sad

Peace: to truly get along and be in a good relationship with someone; being calm and at rest

Peacemakers: those who help others get along

Persecute: to harm and treat very badly because of hatred

Pollen: a flower's powdery substance, often yellow or white; produced by the anther of the flower; when transferred to the stigma, it produces new seeds; insects collect this for food

Pollination: the process by which pollen is transferred from the anther of a flower to the stigma which allows new seeds to be made

Promise: to give your word that you will do something

Pure: clean; to exist without being mixed with other ingredients

Purify: to cleanse or make pure

Punishment: what we receive when we do wrong

Quality: characteristic, feature

Relationship: a connection, like being in the same family

Restored: to be fixed to the way it should be

Repent: to confess you were wrong and to turn away from what you did wrong

Righteous: without sin

Righteousness: having the quality of being righteous

Rival: team you fight against; enemy of similar or equal ability

Sin: to break God's law; choosing our way instead of God's way; disobedience to God; doing or thinking wrong

Wages: what is earned from the work we do

Becky Lane

is a teacher who loves to be outside seeing
God's creation up close. She taught for twelve years before
pursuing writing and illustrating more passionately.
If she is not spending time with family and friends,
she is likely gardening, running, or creating art.

You can find more of Becky's writing on her website www.lifeandlearning365.com.

Ambassador International's mission is to magnify the Lord Jesus Christ
and promote His Gospel through the written word.

For more information about
AMBASSADOR INTERNATIONAL
please visit:
www.ambassador-international.com
www.facebook.com/AmbassadorIntl
@AmbassadorIntl

Thank you for reading this book. Please consider leaving us a review on your social media,
favorite retailer's website, Goodreads, Bookbub, or our website.

Also Available From
AMBASSADOR INTERNATIONAL

Guess How Much God Loves You is the story of seven-year-old Lucy Lu, a colorful, creatively curious first-grader, who is starting to have serious questions about God. How old is He? Does He sleep? What does He do all day? And the biggest one of all—does God love me? After one particularly hard day of being bullied by her classmates at school, Lucy feels like she doesn't matter. She sits with Papa Joe, who has promised to answer her questions about God, launching them onto a journey to discover God's never-changing, never-failing, never-ending love. What follows is a wild adventure through the Bible, where Lucy and her papa find themselves in the middle of each page of the exciting story of God's love and faithfulness for all people throughout all of history.

Sky, a boisterous young pup, and her family are enjoying a day at the lake when they discover a sore in Sky's mouth. A trip to the veterinarian's office soon reveals Sky has cancer. Not giving up hope, Sky's family and friends turn to prayer for her healing.

Although a sensitive topic for children, *Miraculous Sky* is a resource for families going through a similar situation. This uplifting children's book reminds us that we can turn to God for comfort and guidance during difficult times. It also teaches children how to trust God with their needs.